HOW IT WAS

WORKSHOP OF THE WORLD

MID-VICTORIAN BRITAIN

Andrew Lee

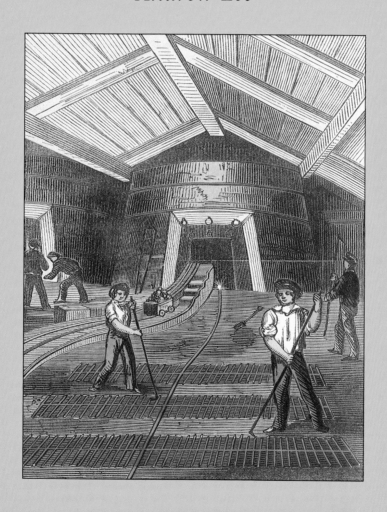

B.T. Batsford Ltd, London

CONTENTS

© Andrew Lee 1993

First published 1993

Typeset by Goodfellow & Egan, Cambridge

and printed in Hong Kong by Colorcraft Ltd

for the publishers
B.T. Batsford Ltd
4 Fitzhardinge Street
London W1H 0AH

ISBN 0 7134 6353 8

A CIP catalogue record for this book is available from the British Library.

The frontispiece shows one of the processes involved in the manufacturing of iron in 1846. In reality, the work involved was dirty, exhausting and very dangerous.

INTRODUCTION

You live in an industrial society. Most of the objects around you have been made in factories using machine tools. Your way of life depends upon high levels of scientific and technical knowledge.

However, if you were able to travel back to the early 1700s, you would see very little that was familiar. Most people worked in agriculture and lived in the countryside. The few articles owned by ordinary people were made by local craftsmen out of simple and natural materials. Life was governed by the rising and the setting of the sun, by the seasons and by the weather. Life for most people was probably cruel, hard and short. There were few medicines. Bad harvests would result in famine. In some circumstances about half of all children born died before reaching the age of five.

The Industrial Revolution turned the world of the 1700s into the world that you know today. This was a great series of changes over many years in the way in which we produced the goods and materials we use for living. The first crude machines began to appear for the production of cheap cotton textiles. New ways were found of making iron, using coke as a fuel and water to power the bellows and blowing cylinders of the blast furnaces. The pottery industry in Staffordshire expanded rapidly. Coal mining expanded to provide fuel for industrial and domestic use, and also for the first steam engines which slowly began to replace water wheels. Goods began to be manufactured in factories instead of in the homes of craftsmen. The factories and their workers were concentrated in new industrial towns such as Manchester, Liverpool and Birmingham.

These industrial changes were accompanied by others, such as the growth of population from 5.5 million in about 1696 to 27.4 million in 1851, the rapid growth in the output of agriculture and a steady rise in the level of overseas trade.

By the 1850s the benefits of the Industrial Revolution were reaching the population at large. Life was still hard, but average national income per head rose by a third between 1850 and 1864. The inventions of the late eighteenth and early nineteenth centuries had given Britain a clear lead over other countries in manufacturing industries. The development of steam railways and shipping brought raw materials from around the world to Britain, where they were manufactured into goods which were then exported for sale. Britain was called the 'Workshop of the World' (an expression first used by Disraeli, in 1838). It was a period of great confidence, during which people believed that science, technology and business could bring about real progress for mankind. This was a period of great engineering achievements, for example in the completion of the mainline railway network. The first proper steps were taken in the provision of proper life-support systems for the new towns: the great Victorian sewerage systems began to be constructed, many of which we still depend on today.

However, by the 1870s other countries, especially Germany and the United States, were having their own industrial revolutions and entering world trade. Britain now faced significant competition and by the end of the century there was even a campaign to put a form of tax on imports. The confidence of mid-century had started to waver!

Introductory Quiz

Do you know?

Who built an iron ship called the *Great Britain* and formed a railway company called the *Great Western?*

What was a steam hammer used for?

What goods did Britain sell to the rest of the world?

Who first invented a way of making cheap steel?

What was the Crystal Palace?

Who was the most famous social reformer of the nineteenth century?

Why was the death rate so high in Victorian cities?

THE GREAT EXHIBITION

The Great Exhibition of 1851 symbolized Britain's position as the Workshop of the World. The idea came from businessmen and manufacturers, who wanted to show off Britain's achievements and win new orders both at home and abroad. The exhibition was also intended to encourage international understanding by 'uniting the industry and art of all the nations of the earth' (*the Royal Commission headed by Prince Albert*), although as it turned out, the exhibits were dominated by British machinery and manufacturers. Other countries had not yet acquired engineering and manufacturing industries that could compete in scale and workmanship.

The exhibition was planned by a committee headed by Prince Albert, the husband of Queen Victoria. Albert had a strong sense of public duty and although the royal family could not interfere in politics, he could lend his support to public affairs such as trade and industry. The planning committee held a competition for the design of an exhibition hall. It did not look as if the competition was going to be a success until Joseph Paxton submitted his remarkable idea. He had been employed by the Duke of Devonshire as a landscape and garden designer. The idea that he came up with was rather like a giant greenhouse. Paxton proposed the use of mass-produced prefabricated cast-iron columns and cross-pieces to support a 'crystal palace' of glass. Paxton's design had the advantage that it could be built rapidly. It also represented the brilliant achievements of mid-Victorian iron-founders and civil engineers. Paxton's design won the competition, although in its final form, the crystal palace acquired a barrel-vaulted main roof. Like many new buildings today, the crystal palace had some stern critics! It was built in Hyde Park, London.

The building was nearly 610 metres long and over 120 metres wide. The iron frame of the building supported nearly 300,000 panes of glass. To gain an impression of what it must have been like, think of a greatly enlarged version of the Palm House at Kew Gardens, which you can still see today. The Crystal Palace enclosed within it some of the elm trees of Hyde Park. Queen Victoria was worried about the fate of the sparrows trapped inside by the construction work. When she asked what could be done about them the Duke of Wellington suggested drily, 'Sparrowhawks, ma'am!'

Inside the great exhibition hall were 19,000 exhibits. Pride of place went to British inventions and machinery including a giant Nasmyth steam hammer and a complete Great Western Railway broad-gauge locomotive. (The rails of the Great Western were set 2.13m apart instead of the usual 1.43m.) Queen Victoria visited the exhibition and wrote in her diary afterwards: 'We remained two hours and a half and I came back quite beaten, and my head bewildered, from the myriads of beautiful and wonderful things, which now quite dazzle one's eyes.'

In 1853–4 the Crystal Palace was moved to Sydenham, Kent, which is now part of south

London. The building remained until 1936 when it was destroyed by fire. All that remains of this symbol of an age are the stone steps and footings in the grounds of the Crystal Palace sports complex.

The Great Exhibition was visited by more than six million people from all over Britain and ran for 141 days. This was made possible by the newly developed railway network. Many of the visitors travelled by cheap excursion trains which made it possible for ordinary people to attend. A point which impressed observers at the time was the way in which 'respectable' members of the working classes mixed with the high and mighty of the land, as they strolled beneath the high-arched ceiling of the exhibition hall. This alarmed some observers such as Colonel Sibthorpe, a Member of Parliament who believed that the presence of foreign visitors and so many members of the working classes would result in 'every species of fraud and immorality'. Other observers thought that the gathering of such numbers would create the opportunity for riot and revolution, but they were proved wrong.

A picture of the exterior of Crystal Palace. The scenes from different countries which surround the painting, emphasize the international aims of the Great Exhibition.

THE GREAT EXHIBITION

Floorplan of the Great Exhibition

Below is a section of the floorplan showing manufacturing goods and engineering tools. The exhibition also contained exhibits such as technical instruments, chemicals, textiles and arts and crafts from around the world. Which categories were the most important?

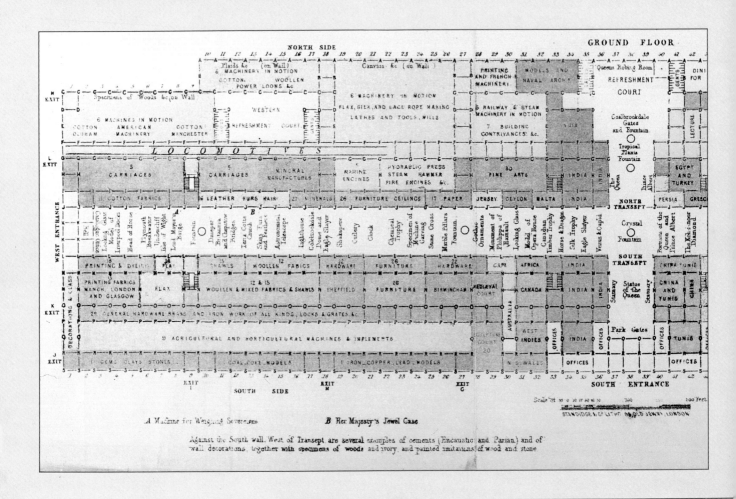

THINGS TO DO

1 Find out more about the life and work of Prince Albert the Prince Consort.

2 See if you can find any material on modern world trade fairs, such as Expo '88 in Brisbane, Australia, and Expo '92 in Seville, Spain.

3 Design a detailed poster advertising a railway excursion to London to visit the Great Exhibition.

CAN YOU REMEMBER ?

What advantages were gained from constructing the Crystal Palace out of cast-iron and glass?

What benefits did the organizing committee hope would be gained from the Exhibition?

The Nasmyth Steam Hammer

This steam hammer is capable of adjustment of power in a degree highly remarkable. While it is possible to obtain enormous impulsive force by its means, it can be so graduated as to descend with power only sufficient to break an egg shell.

(Catalogue of the Great Exhibition 1851)

SPECIMENS FROM MR. PUNCH'S INDUSTRIAL EXHIBITION OF 1850.

(TO BE IMPROVED IN 1851).

Prince Albert attends Punch's preview of the 1851 Great Exhibition   Leech 1850

When you have read this account of the Steam Hammer, have a look at the illustration which appears on page 26. How do you think a visitor to the Great Exhibition might have reacted to an exhibit such as this?

Mr Punch (from the humorous magazine of the same name) reminds Prince Albert that not everybody shares in the wealth of the Workshop of the World. What do you think a 'sweater' is?

The Times reports on the opening day of the Great Exhibition

It was felt to be more than what was seen, or what had been intended. Some saw in it the second and more glorious inauguration of their sovereign; some were more reminded of that day when all ages and climes shall be gathered round the Throne of their Maker.

(*The Times* (2 May 1851))

Which phrases in this description mean (a) the Coronation and (b) Judgement Day? Do you think people *really* compared the Great Exhibition with these two things?

FREE TRADE AND LAISSEZ-FAIRE

In the eighteenth century the government generally discouraged imports by imposing tariffs (taxes) on them. There were also regulations which prevented the export of goods, machinery or inventions which might help foreign competitors. However, as British industry grew during the Industrial Revolution, factory owners wanted to be able to import raw materials and export their manufactured goods without having to pay any tariffs. This is known as Free Trade, and they believed that the government should follow a policy of *laissez-faire* (a French phrase which means 'leave it alone').

The most important source of Free Trade ideas was a book by the influential Scottish economist Adam Smith, called *The Wealth of Nations* (1776). He said that the country as a whole would grow richer if people were allowed to pursue their own economic self-interest – that is, to make, buy or sell whatever they wanted to whomever they wanted without government interference. Smith also argued that *competition* between producers was a good thing because it kept prices down.

These ideas found particular favour among the industrialists and politicians of Lancashire who were led by Richard Cobden and became known as the Manchester School. The cotton manufacturers of Lancashire depended on imported raw materials and on the export of their goods to foreign markets. They wanted Free Trade so that their raw materials would be cheap and their finished goods would be affordable.

By the 1830s and 1840s the front-line supporters of Free Trade, led by Cobden, were the members of the Anti-Corn Law League. They believed that the removal of the import duty on foreign grain would encourage international trade and would make staple foods such as bread cheaper.

When Robert Peel became Prime Minister in 1841 some progress had already been made towards Free Trade. William Huskisson, the member of Parliament for Liverpool, had reduced and simplified the mass of customs laws during his period of office between 1823 and 1827. But he had lost office as a result of a political quarrel within the Tory Party and had then been killed in an accident on the opening day of the Liverpool and Manchester Railway in 1830. However, in 1841 a Parliamentary Select Committee on Import Duties came out strongly in favour of further steps towards Free Trade. The stage was now set for Sir Robert Peel, as Prime Minister, to embark upon a whole series of reforms. These included reforms of taxation, banking and currency. Peel's reforms helped to provide many of the right conditions for the growth of Britain's prosperity as the Workshop of the World. Most famously, Peel continued the process of reducing import duties on both raw materials and manufactured goods. In 1845 the duties on 450 articles were abolished completely. Then in 1846 came the greatest symbolic move of all: with public opinion running in favour of Free Trade as a result of the activities of the Anti-Corn Law League, and with a terrible famine in Ireland as a result of the potato blight, Peel decided to repeal [withdraw] the Corn Laws.

Peel's actions split his own party because many of its members were grain farmers who feared overseas competition. Peel fell from power in 1846 and then died as a result of a riding accident in Hyde Park in 1850, but his work was carried on by one of his followers, William Gladstone. Step by step, as circumstances permitted, tariffs were reduced or removed, until the whole process reached its climax in 1860. In that year the Cobden Free Trade Treaty was made with France. Gladstone was Chancellor of the Exchequer in the administration of Palmerston, and introduced a budget which removed all remaining forms of government control on trade with the exception of tariffs on 48 articles.

Free Trade had triumphed and between 1850 and 1873 the Workshop of the World appeared to thrive on the achievements of Huskisson, Peel and Gladstone. Exports soared from £83.4m in 1850 to £244.1m in 1870. It certainly looked as if freedom from government restraints meant that the enterprise of Britain's industrialists and businessmen was being allowed to flourish and that as the country grew wealthier it was sucking in more 'luxury' goods such as tea, coffee and sugar from overseas as well.

A cartoon of Gladstone from Vanity Fair *(1879)*

FREE TRADE AND LAISSEZ-FAIRE

Was the freedom from government restraints a triumph of *laissez-faire*? As far as trade was concerned, the answer for the time being was probably: yes. But in other areas the involvement of government was growing. During the 1830s and 1840s governments realized that problems such as bad working conditions and the employment of young children could only be solved by government action. Laws were passed to regulate working conditions (see page 37.) and soon governments were involved in matters such as public health and education as well. By the 1870s the enforcement of laws on such matters by Her Majesty's Inspectors was common, although not always effective. Britain was on the path towards becoming a collectivist state, that is one where the government assumes a responsibility to solve certain problems which cannot be solved by individuals alone.

'Peel's cheap bread shop'

This cartoon shows one possible result of Sir Robert Peel's abolition of the Corn Laws. 'Russell' was Lord John Russell, a Whig politician who was a late convert to the abolition of the Corn Laws, and who failed to form a Government when invited by Queen Victoria in 1845.

Why might the abolition of the Corn Laws have made bread cheaper?
How would this help the 'Workshop of the World'?
Using the information in this chapter and on page 17, say whether the price of grain for bread fell, and if so, when?

PEEL'S CHEAP BREAD SHOP,
OPENED JANUARY 22, 1846.

THINGS TO DO

Read page 40 on the End of the Workshop of the World and then write two imaginary letters to *The Times* about what the government is doing to encourage trade, one from the point of view of a cotton factory owner in 1838, and one from the point of view of a wheat farmer in 1885.

CAN YOU REMEMBER ?

Who first wrote about the ideas of Free Trade and laissez-faire?

Who was the politician who completed the progress to Free Trade?

Richard Cobden and the Case for Free Trade

Free Trade! What is it? Why, breaking down the barriers that separate nations; Those barriers behind which nestle the feelings of pride, revenge, hatred and jealousy, which every now and then burst their bounds, and deluge whole countries with blood; those feelings which nourish the poison of war and conquest, which assert that without conquest we can have no trade . . .

(Richard Cobden, from a speech following the formation of the Anti-Corn Law League, 1838)

Cobden's speech makes a *moral* case for Free Trade; can you explain briefly what he was saying?

What *economic* arguments were there for Free Trade?

Some evidence about the Effects of Free Trade

Thirty years ago England had almost a monopoly of the manufacturing industries of the world; she produced everything in excess of her consumption, other nations produced comparatively nothing. The world was obliged to buy from her, because it could not buy anywhere else.

(Edward Sullivan, in *The Nineteenth Century* August 1881, quoted in Patrick Rooke *The Age of Dickens*)

. . . it is the opinion of this House that the improved condition of the country, and especially of the industrious classes, is mainly the result of recent legislation, which has established the principle of unrestricted competition and abolished taxes imposed for the purposes of protection, and has thereby diminished the cost and increased the abundance of the principle articles of food to the people.

That it is the opinion of this House that that policy firmly maintained and prudently extended, will best enable the industry of the country to bear its burdens, and will thereby most surely promote the welfare and contentment of the people.

(Resolution of the House of Commons, 23 November 1852)

What do these extracts suggest was the result of Free Trade? Can you think of any reasons for being cautious about any of these pieces of evidence?

CHECK YOUR UNDERSTANDING

What is the opposite to Free Trade?

What might encourage a country to *abandon* Free Trade?

THE RAILWAY AGE

The canals and turnpike roads of the eighteenth century did not fully answer the transport needs of the Workshop of the World, being slow, inefficiently managed, and with restricted access. The answer to these difficulties had been steadily evolving in the coal-mining areas of Northumberland and South Wales. It was the steam-hauled railway, which reached its basic form with the opening of the Liverpool and Manchester Railway in 1830. Its engineer, George Stephenson, supported the idea that locomotive steam engines could be used to haul a regular service of both passenger and goods trains. People wondered whether the idea would really work, or whether the worst predictions of the critics would come true: would the bridges and embankments collapse, would human beings suffocate when travelling at speeds of 30 miles per hour and more? Then, as the Liverpool and Manchester's receipts came rolling in, the first trunk lines [lines between major cities] were embarked upon. Between 1833 and 1835 the London and Birmingham, London and Southampton, Grand Junction, and Great Western lines were authorized by Parliament, to be followed by the first 'railway mania' of 1836–7 in which a further 1,500 miles of railway were approved. In the second railway mania of 1845–7 the country was gripped by a feverish desire to build and invest in the wonder of the age. A further 9,000 miles of line were authorized, Parliament agreeing to 650 separate railway acts between 1845 and 1848.

By the early 1850s over 6,000 miles of railway had been built and most major towns in England were served. By 1870, 13,500 miles of railway were open and the main railway network was complete.

The speed of this development was so rapid that it can be called a railway revolution. The effects of this railway revolution in creating and shaping the Workshop of the World were immense. The construction of new canals virtually ceased, and by 1848 the last mail coach was withdrawn (although vast amounts of horse-drawn transport were still needed to fetch and carry for the railway companies). The faster and cheaper transport offered by the railways meant that new goods travelled to markets that they might not have reached before, and people who might never have travelled away from their home towns found it possible to move around for business, in search of work or even for pleasure. Half a million people travelled on the London and Birmingham line in 1838; in 1845 the same company carried a million passengers.

The economic impact of railways was twofold. Railways made economic growth possible by providing transport, but railways were also great consumers of capital, material and labour. For example, 18 per cent of UK iron output probably went into railways between 1844 and 1851, and the 1851 census listed 34,306 railway labourers and 14,559 railway officials.

Railways affected technology by encouraging all areas of mechanical, civil and even electrical engineering. A good example is the development of the electric telegraph for signalling purposes and communication.

Railways had a financial effect by encouraging the growth of the London Stock Exchange, which became the centre for railway speculation. They also made it possible for mid-Victorian farmers to practise the methods of High Farming (see page 16).

The Railway Station *by William Frith. This painting shows the bustle of Paddington Station in the early days of the Great Western Railway. How would you describe the passengers and their luggage? Do you think that these were the only type of people to travel by train?*

THE RAILWAY AGE

The railways brought more than just economic and technological change. By the 1850s they were bringing a social revolution as well. The 1844 Railway Act compelled railway companies to provide at least one train each day to carry third class passengers at a fare of no more than one penny per mile. Thus rail travel started to move people around and bring them together. It also made them more aware of how other social classes lived. It is therefore not surprising that a supporter of railways could call them 'a device for making the world smaller', whilst a staunch enemy of change such as Colonel Charles Sibthorpe MP could say that 'next to civil war, railways are the greatest curse to the country'.

Can you explain why Charles Sibthorpe should feel this way?

The Economic Impact of Railways

And along the iron veins that traverse the frame of our country, beat and flow the fiery pulses of its exertions, hotter and faster every hour. All vitality is concentrated through those throbbing arteries into the central cities.

(John Ruskin *The Seven Lamps of Architecture*, 1849)

What picture is Ruskin creating when he describes railways as 'throbbing arteries'?

The Social Impact of the Railways

Companies [must] provide upon such new Lines of Railway, as a minimum of third-class accommodation, one Train at least each way on every week-day, by which there shall be the ordinary stations, in carriages provided with seats and protected from the weather, at a speed not less than 12 miles an hour including stoppages, and fares not exceeding a penny per mile . . . Children under Three years being conveyed without extra charge; and Children from Three to Twelve years at half-price.

(From the Report of the Select Committee on Railways, 1844, and implemented by an Act of Parliament)

'You came by the railroad?' inquired Lord de Mowbray mournfully, of Lady Marney.
'From Marham; about ten miles from us,' replied her ladyship.
'A great revolution!'
'Isn't it?'
'I fear it has a very dangerous tendency to equality,' said his lordship, shaking his head; [. . .] 'Equality, Lady Marney, equality is not our metier [business or concern]. If we nobles do not make a stand against the levelling spirit of the age, I am at a loss to know who will fight the battle. You may depend upon it that these railroads are very dangerous things.'

(Benjamin Disraeli *Sybil*, 1845)

Can you explain in your own words why Lord de Mowbray should think 'these railroads are very dangerous things'?

The Liverpool to Manchester Line 1831

Compare the two kinds of carriages on these trains,
and explain why they are so different.

HIGH FARMING

The third quarter of the nineteenth century was a good time for farmers as well as for manufacturers. The growing population meant that there was a steadily increasing demand for food. Rising wages among the growing numbers of urban workers meant that people could afford a slightly more varied and substantial diet. Railways and canals helped to open up new markets; beef producers in Scotland could even send their cattle to London. At the same time the railways could deliver fertilizer, machinery and fuel more cheaply to country areas.

There was little foreign competition. It had been feared that the repeal of the Corn Laws (see page 8) would result in a flood of cheap imported grain, but this did not happen until the mid 1870s. In the meantime Britain could eat all that could be produced, especially in meat and dairy products, and although grain prices fell slightly from their 1846 level, the prices of other agricultural products generally rose by between 20 and 50 per cent.

In these circumstances farmers were anxious to apply new techniques which would enable them to produce more, or allow them to employ fewer workers. The so-called Agricultural Revolution of the eighteenth century had already seen improvements such as selective breeding, new crop rotations, and more sensible organization of land holdings as a result of enclosure. By the 1850s farmers were increasingly interested in more scientific methods, labour-saving machinery and

heavy capital investment in land improvement. This was what Sir James Caird called 'High Farming'.

The spread of scientific methods was made possible by a number of developments. In 1838 the Royal Agricultural Society was founded and it started to publish a regular journal. In 1840 Justus von Liebig published *Organic Chemistry in its Application to Agriculture and Physiology*, a widely read book which summed up the state of knowledge on the chemistry of plant nutrition. In 1843 the agricultural research station was founded by Sir John Lawes at Rothamsted and in 1845 Cirencester Agricultural College was established. There were numerous popular publications available to farmers who wanted to learn the most recent developments, and text books such as Low's *Elements of Practical Agriculture* and Youatt's the *Complete Grazier* ran to many editions. Through these channels information flowed about chemical fertilizers such as phosphates (first used in 1795), guano (sea-bird droppings) and nitrates from South America, potash (imported from Germany from 1860 onwards), sulphate of ammonia, basic slag (from the iron industry) and even crushed bones and blood.

The Royal Agricultural Society's Journal could also report on the many new machines available. We sometimes tend to imagine that the age of mechanized agriculture started in the eighteenth century with Jethro Tull and his horse-drawn seed drill. But the practical application of machines to farming did not really come until the nineteenth century. Only then were the engineering skills and materials available to make the machines sufficiently light for use on the land. Even in the early part of the nineteenth century it was probably human labour rather than machinery which was the basis of

The Emigrant's Last Sight of Home *by Richard Redgrave (1859). The painting shows another effect of labour-saving machinery: agricultural labourers are leaving their homes to go abroad because they can no longer make a living on the land. From 1840, at least 100,000 people left the United Kingdom altogether each year.*

farming: the census of 1831 showed that the number of families on the land had actually risen since 1801. However, by the 1850s there seems to have been a flood of new implements available. Steam threshing was already common by 1850. At the Great Exhibition there were many agricultural machines on show, including the McCormick reaper from America. Seed drills, mechanical cultivators and improved ploughs were widely advertised. At the Gloucester Show in 1853 there were 2000 mechanical exhibits, and at Chester in 1858 the Royal Agricultural Society examined 89 different makes of threshing machine. Mobile steam engines were used as a source of power and farmers were encouraged to invest in labour-saving devices by the rising cost of wages and laws which restricted the employment of children (although a McCormick reaper still required a team of 12 to operate it; a modern arable farm might be run by only two or three men in total). Sir James Caird estimated that by the 1870s there were 40,000 reapers in use. There is a report of a Wiltshire farmer who in 1859 grubbed up his hedges and reduced his number of fields from 36 to 9, purchased a 14 horse power steam engine, sold off his seven teams of oxen and claimed to have reduced his cultivation costs by one third.

Another exhibit at the Great Exhibition was Fowler's mole plough. This machine made it possible to lay drains in the soil through a narrow slit at the surface. Effective drainage of the soil could improve crop yields considerably. The mole plough, together with the cheap machine-made clay pipes produced by John Reade, encouraged farmers to invest large amounts of money in improvements. In some cases the government helped by providing low interest loans. It was estimated that during this 'Golden Age' of British agriculture (a phrase used at the time by Lord Ernle) more than £24 million was spent on drainage, building and fertilizer.

However, one has to be careful in judging the value and importance of High Farming. For the new techniques to be really worthwhile farms had to be larger than 300 acres, but only about one third of farmland was occupied by farms of this size. It has also been argued that too much money was spent in the search for technical efficiency at a time when prices were high and markets were growing.

HIGH FARMING

What was the life of the farm labourer like in this period? Farm work has always been hard and relatively low-paid. However, wages appear to have been rising: in 1850 they stood at roughly nine shillings and sixpence (47½p) per week and rose to about twelve shillings (60p) per week in 1870, although it has to be remembered that food prices were also rising. New methods and machinery required more skilled labour and this had to be paid for, even if the total number of hands required might be less. A modification in the Poor Law in 1865 encouraged a general improvement in rural housing by the 1880s. Nevertheless, farm workers in less prosperous areas or on the smaller unimproved farms might still live in squalor which contrasted grimly with the conditions enjoyed even by the farm animals of the great estates.

Evidence of Progress in the 'Golden Age of British Agriculture'

... Meadows began to appear where swamps existed before; plantations dotted the country where heather and whins [scrubland or gorse] had formerly been; new farm buildings were erected, and old ones renewed; straight fences were seen in direct contrast with the zig-zag hedges of the inclosure; the varied stages of cultivation diversified and improved the aspect of the whole country; the area of arable land was nearly, if not fully, doubled in extent; and along with all these changes the habits of the people were converted from the listless lounge of the half-shepherd, half-husbandman [man who grows crops], to the active, industrious, and persevering qualities of the agriculturalist, who has now been taught to feel that the welfare of himself and family must depend entirely on his own energies ...

(William Dickinson, 'Essay on the Agriculture of East Cumberland' 1853, quoted in Pamela Horn, *Life and Labour in Rural England 1760–1850*)

Agriculture and the Railways

Cattle and sheep for the Smithfield Monday market had to leave their homes the previous Wednesday or Thursday week. Such a long drift [journey], particularly in hot weather, caused a great waste of meat. The heavy stall-fed cattle of East Norfolk suffered severely. The average loss on such bullocks was considered to be 4 stones of 14 lb, while the best yearling sheep are proved to have lost 6 lb of mutton and 4 lb of tallow ... Stock now leave on Saturday and are in the salesmen's layers [stables or barns] that evening, fresh for the metropolitan market on Monday morning.

(James Caird describes one of the beneficial effects of railways on agriculture in *English Agriculture in 1850–51*)

Cattle being transported on the Great Northern Railway. How did this help to prevent 'a great waste of meat?'

The Steam-Powered Thresher

The most remarkable feature in agricultural operations of the present day is undoubtedly the rapid introduction and use of small portable steam engines for agricultural purposes, especially noticeable in connection with the combined threshing, straw-stacking and dressing machines, unknown until the last two years, on account of the non-efficiency of 'horse-power' application to the working of such apparatus.

(From the catalogue of the Great Exhibition)

THINGS TO DO

1 Try to find a picture of a machine such as a **McCormick Reaper**, or a portable steam engine, and then design and write an advertising pamphlet explaining its use and benefits.

2 Find out from your library which different chemicals plants need for vigorous growth, and how they can be provided.

CHECK YOUR UNDERSTANDING

Why would farmers in the mid-nineteenth century want to introduce new methods?

Which farmers would be the first to adopt new methods?

What reasons might there be for other farmers being slow to take up new ways of farming?

What various signs of progress or improvements are shown in the extracts on these pages?

What advantages did steam-powered machinery bring to agriculture?

CAN YOU REMEMBER ?

Who first used the term 'High Farming', and what did it mean?

Don't put all your eggs in one basket

The safe course for the English agriculturalist is to endeavour, by increasing his livestock, to render himself less dependent on corn, while he at the same time enriches his farm by their manure, and is thus enabled to grow heavier crops at less comparative cost.

(James Caird, *English Agriculture in 1850–51*)

Read page 41 in the chapter on 'The End of the Workshop of the World'. What happened to farmers who did not heed Caird's advice?

IRON AND STEEL

Iron production had increased a hundred-fold between 1700 and 1830. 'Iron-mad' John Wilkinson had demonstrated the many uses to which cast iron could be put, including an iron boat and water pipes, and he also developed one of the earliest precision machine tools, a lathe for boring out cannon. In 1783 Henry Cort developed the puddling and rolling process by which large quantities of pig iron (the crude form of iron which comes from a blast furnace) could be further refined into wrought iron. Wrought iron is a more malleable and resilient form of iron which was used in the first half of the nineteenth century to make machinery, railway lines, wheels, cranks, ship's plates and could also be used for construction purposes such as bridge building. Steel (iron which has been further refined and then had carefully measured amounts of other chemicals such as carbon and manganese put back into it) was produced only in small amounts and used for items such as cutting tools and watch springs; it was too expensive to be used on a larger scale.

By 1850 the Workshop of the World made half of the world's pig iron, and iron and steel represented 16 per cent of Britain's exports. 142,000 tons of iron were shipped abroad in 1850, a figure which rose to 950,000 tons in 1875. Wrought iron was the dominant material in 1850. Total iron output for that year was around 2 million tons but only about 60,000 tons was converted to steel. The key worker in iron-producing towns such as Sheffield was the puddler. He stirred the iron in the furnace to burn off the impurities. The iron was then hauled out and hammered or squeezed between rollers to produce wrought iron. The puddler's work was very hard and dangerous; the life-expectancy of Sheffield puddlers in the late 1860s was only 31 years. Cast iron was much in use also. It was employed to make the frame for the Crystal Palace (see page 4) and was suitable for the manufacture of a wide variety of domestic articles such as pots, pans and fire grates. The ingenuity of the Victorians in making so many things out of iron was revealed at the Great Exhibition.

In 1856 a professional inventor called Henry Bessemer revealed his process for making cheap steel in large quantities. Mild steel is harder and stronger than wrought iron, but it is still malleable and therefore can be used for a wide variety of manufacturing and constructional purposes.

Bessemer blew air at high pressure through molten iron contained within a vessel called a converter. The air burned off the excessive impurities in the iron in a spectacular shower of sparks and flame. The length of the 'blow' could be varied to leave the right amount of carbon to make mild steel, or other chemicals could be added to make other types of special steel. The steel could then be cast or rolled directly into the shapes required without the need for any further forging.

Bessemer's process cut the price of steel by about a half, but there was no immediate rush by the iron producers to abandon wrought iron and turn to the new product. There were various reasons for this. Bessemer's process could not remove phosphorus from iron, but most British iron ores contained a high proportion of phosphorus. Consequently Bessemer steel could only be made using the non-phosphoric ores of Cumberland and Cleveland, or by importing iron ore from Sweden or Spain. The market was conservative: it would take time for steel to demonstrate its superiority over wrought iron; the Board of Trade did not permit its use in bridge construction until 1877. Bessemer undercut the price charged by his rivals for high quality tool steel, but he charged a high licence fee to allow other people to use his process, and so Bessemer steel was still more expensive than wrought iron. On top of this, the iron producers were reluctant to change their ways.

Nevertheless the advantages of steel were clear: for example, the first steel railway lines were laid on the London and North Western Railway at Camden in 1862. Before long, further progress was being made in steel making. In 1867, Sir William Siemen's open hearth furnace was used to make mild steel more cheaply and more easily than by the Bessemer process. In an open hearth furnace, waste heat from the furnace itself was used to pre-heat the incoming gas fuel, which burned across the surface of the liquid iron at ever-increasing temperatures until the impurities were burned off. It was a more controllable and more energy-efficient process, which could also use a proportion of scrap steel, as was discovered in France by Martins, whose name is often linked with that of Siemens. Siemens set up the Siemens Steel Company at Landore, South Wales, in 1869. By 1873 it was producing 1000 tons of steel per week and the Siemens process began to overhaul Bessemer production.

Then in 1878 Sidney Gilchrist Thomas, a police court clerk who dabbled in chemistry, produced the solution to the problem of how to make steel from phosphoric iron. He developed the *basic* process in which the furnace or converter is lined with dolomitic limestone (rock containing calcium and magnesium) which absorbs the phosphorus (and also produces a useful agricultural fertilizer, basic slag).

During the 1870s the railways and the shipyards made the decisive change to using steel. In 1870 Britain's steel production was 300,000 tons; in 1880 it reached 1.25m tons (although steel production did not actually overtake iron until 1918). In 1871 Britain produced 40 per cent of the world's steel, but it is important to note that Germany and the United States, both of which had large deposits of phosphoric ores, were far quicker to take advantage of the basic method and by 1900 had overtaken British production (see page 40). The century ended with the construction of some of the great masterpieces of engineering in steel, such as the Forth railway bridge.

The engraving shows a block of pig iron being rolled in a furnace. Why would iron-making be a dangerous occupation?

IRON AND STEEL

Bessemer's Converter

Henry Bessemer describes what happened when his converter was first used to make steel:

> The silicon had been quietly consumed; and the oxygen, next uniting with the carbon, sent up an ever-increasing stream of sparks and a voluminous white flame. Then followed a succession of mild explosions, throwing molten slags and splashes of metal high in the air, the apparatus becoming a veritable volcano in a state of active eruption. No one could approach the converter to turn off the blast, and some low, flat roofs close at hand were in danger of being set on fire by the shower of red-hot matter falling on them. All this was a revelation to me, as I had in no way anticipated such violent results. However, in ten minutes more the eruption had ceased, the flame died down, and the process was complete.

(Quoted in *Machines, Money and Men* by D.P. Titley)

Q

What was it that caused such a spectacular effect?

What was happening?

CAN YOU REMEMBER ?

What is the difference between pig iron, wrought iron and steel?

What, briefly, were the main achievements of John Wilkinson, Henry Cort, Henry Bessemer, Sir William Siemens and Sidney Gilchrist Thomas?

THINGS TO DO

(You will probably need to ask your teacher to arrange these activities.)

1 Ask a teacher from your school's Science Department to explain the chemistry involved in the smelting, refining and production of iron and steel.

2 Visit your school's CDT Department and ask to see processes such as forging and casting. (It will probably not be possible to see iron being cast, but it is usually possible to see aluminium being cast in a school engineering shop.) See if you can identify the different forms of iron and steel that are used in the construction of your home, your school and the items in them.

The manufacture of Bessemer steel, showing the converters at work.

The Landore Siemens Steelworks in Wales

Most steelworks were built next to coal mines and
rivers or canals. Can you explain why?

CHECK YOUR UNDERSTANDING

How is steel made?

Why was wrought iron the
favoured material in Britain
until at least the 1860s?

What factors eventually
enabled steel to take over
from wrought iron?

MACHINE TOOLS & ENGINEERING

Before the Industrial Revolution, metal goods were made in small numbers by local craftsmen to many different sizes and specifications. However, two things happened during the Industrial Revolution: firstly, many new and more complicated machines were invented; secondly, new tools and techniques for making the machines were developed. These new tools were known as 'machine tools', devices such as lathes and milling machines which could manufacture large numbers of items to the same dimensions and quality.

Particular engineers became famous for their mechanical inventions and they began to standardize their products, that is they consistently made the parts of their machines to the same dimensions. Henry Bessemer was able to get different parts of the same machinery made independently in Manchester, Glasgow, Liverpool and London. With time it became possible to interchange spare parts easily because of this standardization, although Britain in fact lagged behind the United States, where Eli Whitney had introduced standardized spare parts in the manufacture of guns at the end of the eighteenth century. Nevertheless it was British engineers who led the way and by the 1850s, the manufacturers of

Brunel's ship the Great Eastern *was intended to carry 4,000 passengers and 3,000 tons of cargo. She was constructed of iron and driven by paddle wheels, propellers and sails set on six masts.*

Leeds, Manchester and Birmingham were supplying steam hammers, machine tools and railway locomotives to markets as far away as Russia, Australia, India and the United States.

A famous cradle for the development of engineering was the works of Joseph Bramah in London. Among Bramah's personal achievements were the manufacture of the gates of Marble Arch and the invention, in 1784, of an unpickable lock which remained undefeated until the Great Exhibition. Bramah's pupil Henry Maudsley invented a screw-cutting lathe and the machine tools necessary to mass-produce pully blocks for ships. Another pupil of Bramah was Joseph Clement, who invented the domestic water tap.

Maudsley trained James Nasmyth, whose most famous invention was the steam hammer. This was developed in 1839 to forge the huge propellor shaft of Brunel's steam ship the *Great Britain*. The steam hammer, proudly displayed at the Great Exhibition, could deliver a blow of many tons, or be regulated (so it was claimed) to crack an egg shell.

Another of Maudsley's pupils was Joseph Whitworth, who was greatly interested in precision engineering and standardization. At the Great Exhibition he exhibited a micrometer capable of measuring a millionth of an inch, and in an exhibition of 1862 he displayed a massive drilling machine. In 1880 he eventually persuaded the Board of Trade to adopt a nationwide standard of measurements, especially for screw threads. However, it took a long while before all the talented and inventive individuals in the engineering industry would work to the same standards; despite competition from the mass-produced products of Germany and the United States they claimed that standardization was unnecessary.

A particular branch of engineering in which the British reigned supreme by the end of the nineteenth century was shipbuilding. However, wooden sailing vessels still held sway until the 1850s. American-built softwood ships were cheap and well constructed; the early steam boats had little cargo capacity because their hungry engines required so much coal to be carried (three quarters of the cargo capacity of the Cunard line's Britannia was allotted to carrying fuel).

The Great Eastern *under construction. The small boats in the front of the picture give some idea of the massive size of the ship.*

What brought about the change to metal construction and steam power was the work of pioneers in Britain such as Brunel, the availability of cheaper wrought iron and mild steel, the development of the more economical compound steam engine which could extract more work from a given amount of steam, and the opening up of routes such as the Suez Canal (1869) which were shorter and favoured vessels which could proceed under their own power.

The race to be first across the Atlantic by steam power was narrowly won by the *Sirius* in 1838, which only beat Brunel's *Great Western* by a matter of about four hours, despite a three days' head start. Brunel's inventiveness led him on to construct the *Great Britain*, launched in 1843. The first ship to be constructed completely from iron, she was driven by propellers, and she also had a double bottom and watertight bulkheads. Unfortunately this did not stop her from going aground on the Irish coast in 1846, or again being wrecked on the Falklands, but she has proved so tough that the hull has been returned to Bristol and is now restored and on view.

Despite the fate of Brunel's designs, the advantages of iron-built steamships were increasingly obvious. The Cunard Steamship Company had been awarded the contract for the North Atlantic postal service in 1839, because of its regular schedules. Iron hulls were stronger and lighter than comparable wooden ones and the advantage was even greater once cheap steel became available, although it was not until the 1870s that the switch from wrought iron to steel was made.

The switch to iron construction had brought about a change in the location of the major shipyards. The Thames and the Tyne had been the main locations for the construction of wooden ships; even Brunel's *Great Eastern*, his greatest ship, launched in 1858, had been constructed on the Thames at Milwall (where it had to be launched sideways because of its great length). But with the arrival of iron and steel construction the shipyards clearly had to be sited near to the coalfields and iron industry; consequently Tyneside, Wearside, Clydeside and Barrow came to dominate.

The British shipbuilding industry had become such a world leader that at the battle of Tsushima Bay during the Russo-Japanese war of 1904–5 both sides fought with warships made by Vickers at Barrow.

MACHINE TOOLS & ENGINEERING

'Enormous Impulsive Force' – Nasmyth's Steam Hammer

Study the illustration below carefully. Can you work out how the machine works? If you are stuck, find out first of all how a normal steam engine operates.

What sort of item is being made by this steam hammer?

Labour saving

Sir Joseph Whitworth was, by 1851, the most important machine-tool maker in Britain. At the Great Exhibition he had twenty-three exhibits, including lathes, planing machines and drills. In 1856 he wrote about the advantages of using machines:

Thirty years ago the cost of labour for facing a surface of cast iron by chipping and filing by hand was 12 shillings per square foot; the same work is done by the planing machine at a cost for labour of less than 1 penny per square foot.

What would be the advantage to a manufacturer of using a machine tool such as a planing machine?

Standardization

The introduction of Whitworth's standardization of screw threads had a great impact on British industry.

Now every marine engine and every locomotive in this country has the same screw for every given diameter. His system . . . has been adopted throughout the world, wherever engines and machinery are manufactured, the dies for producing the whole series having been originally furnished from his works at Manchester.

(From *Creators of the Age of Steel* by W.T. Jeans, 1885, quoted in *An Economic History of Britain, Free Trade and Steel* by J.H. Clapham)

How might the use of Whitworth's standard measurements for items such as screw threads encourage the sale of British machinery at home and abroad?

THINGS TO DO

1 Go to your CDT department and ask to see and use a micrometer.

2 Watch a machine tool such as a capstan lathe being used.

3 If you live in the London area, visit the Science Museum, which contains examples of many of the machines mentioned in this chapter; most provincial cities also have similar museums.

4 If you live in the west of England, visit the Clifton suspension bridge and *S.S. Great Britain*, two examples of Brunel's genius, both located in Bristol.

5 See if your school or local library has any more material on the life and achievement of Brunel; make a full list of his achievements which can still be seen.

CHECK YOUR UNDERSTANDING

What is a 'machine tool'?

Of what use is a machine tool in manufacturing industry?

Why did it take longer than you might expect for iron-hulled and steam-driven ships to replace wooden sailing ships?

CAN YOU REMEMBER ?

What is the word used to describe the manufacture of machine parts according to commonly agreed dimensions and specifications?

Can you think of any modern examples of this?

What were the achievements of Bramah, Maudslay and Whitworth?

SELF HELP

By the 1850s, the economic benefits of industrialization had begun to reach ordinary people and the rising prosperity of many skilled workers meant that some of them now had the right to vote. Consequently attention switched to ways in which people could help themselves and make the capitalist system operate for their own benefit. Mid-Victorian England was therefore the era of 'Self Help'.

Self Help was the title of a book published in 1859 by Samuel Smiles, an Edinburgh doctor. He said that people had a moral obligation to look after themselves and that the only answer to poverty was hard work. The ideas of Samuel Smiles were not much comfort to those who were too weak to be able to help themselves, but for skilled workers who were in a strong bargaining position, self help was a real possibility.

A good example of self help in operation was the New Model Trades Unions, the first of which was the Amalgamated Society of Engineers, founded in 1851. These were unions of skilled craftsmen who earned high wages and could afford high subscription rates. They employed full-time officials such as Robert Applegarth of the Carpenters and William Allan of the Engineers. These were educated and moderate men who were in a good position to negotiate with employers. Many of these unions established central offices in London. Among the advantages of membership were forms of insurance such as sickness benefit. The New Model Unions seldom resorted to strikes, firstly because they did not need to and secondly because they did not want to put their insurance funds at risk.

Another example of self help was the Co-operative Movement. This was started by the Rochdale Pioneers of Toad Lane, Rochdale, in 1844. The Co-operative Movement certainly owed something to the ideas of Robert Owen, but the activities of the Rochdale Pioneers were rooted in sound business sense and enterprise. The Pioneers put their savings together and started a small shop which sold goods of decent quality at fair prices (in those days it was not at all unusual for the goods in shops to be adulterated; for example chalk was mixed in with flour, and sawdust added to coffee). Other people could join the Pioneers' Co-operative Society, and at the end of the year any profits were either ploughed back into the business or shared out as a dividend among the members. Working people were making capitalism work for them. By 1851 there were 130 Co-operative Societies and before long there were to be wholesaling and manufacturing co-operatives as well. The Co-operative Movement was to become a major force in society, especially in the Midlands and North, giving many ordinary people the chance to participate in democratic management.

Underpinning the whole range of self help activity were the friendly societies. These ranged from local village and trade clubs, right the way up to

very large organizations such as the Manchester Unity of Oddfellows. The friendly societies provided both social activities and social welfare (for example sickness insurance) for their members, and by the early 1870s they had some four million members.

Nor was the government without a part to play in self help. In 1861 the Post Office Savings Bank was created by Gladstone, at that stage Chancellor of the Exchequer, and he was very impressed by the numbers of ordinary people who made deposits.

Certificates of Trade Union Membership like these, were intended to inspire and unite all those who became members.

SELF HELP

In the late 1860s, demands for the extension of the franchise [right to vote] were revived. A National Reform League was established and in 1866 it held a mass meeting in Hyde Park. There was some trouble, and some railings were pushed down, but the political leaders of the day were convinced by all the examples of self help that the better-off workers could be trusted with the right to vote. In 1867 the Second Reform Act was passed by a Conservative government. It gave the right to vote to all male householders in the borough constituencies and created nearly a million new voters: Britain had taken the first real step towards becoming a democracy. In 1872 the secret ballot was introduced, and in 1874 the first two truly working class MPs were elected.

THINGS TO DO

1 This chapter has touched on many different issues. Follow up the stories of the 1832 and 1867 Reform Acts and find out what further Parliamentary Reform took place in the late nineteenth century as well; when did women gain the right to vote?

2 See what you can learn about your local modern-day 'Co-op'. Design an informative poster, either for the first meeting of a new Co-operative Society or for a meeting of the National Reform League.

CHECK YOUR UNDERSTANDING

What are strikes, lock-outs and blacklists?

Why would skilled workers be in a good position to bargain with their employers?

Working Class Respectability

We now come to the Rochdale District Co-operative Corn Mill Society, which does a large business. It has a capital of 60,000£ and turns over 164,000£ per annum. It has also a committee of eleven, but neither the president, nor treasurer, nor secretary, nor any one of this committee has a borough vote. . . Then there is the Rochdale Co-operative Manufacturing Society, which has more than 1,500 members or shareholders, and a capital of 109,000£. . . This society is also managed by a committee of eleven, of whom three have borough votes, and two have county votes. But of these five voters only one (a mechanic) is a 'working-man' in the usual sense. . . Now, the total capital of these societies is 227,246£, the whole of which has been contributed, or nearly so, by the working men of Rochdale . . .

Now what is taking place in Rochdale societies is occurring in greater or less degree in all the societies, of which there are five or six hundred throughout the country . . .

You have 1,000,000 electors now, and there are 8,000,000 of grown men in the United Kingdom; can you say that only 1,000,000 shall have votes and that all the rest are to remain excluded? Is the thing possible?

(John Bright MP, Rochdale mill owner, speaking in the debate on the second reading of the 1866 Reform Bill quoted in D.G. Wright *Democracy and Reform*)

In this extract, John Bright was arguing that a greater number of ordinary men should be given the right to vote. On what did he base his argument?

Samuel Smiles (Cartoon from Vanity Fair *1882). Why did his ideas seem to offer real opportunities for skilled workers in mid-Victorian England?*

Q

Why is Rochdale important in the history of attempts by working people to 'help themselves'?

What words would you use to describe the Rochdale District Co-operative Corn Mill Society and the Rochdale Co-operative Manufacturing Society?

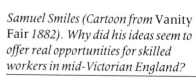

CAN YOU REMEMBER ?

Who was the author of **Self Help***?*

Who set up the first Co-operative Society, when and where?

VICTORIAN CITIES

The most dramatic changes which took place in nineteenth-century Britain concerned the size and distribution of the population. It had trebled between 1750 and 1851, reaching 27.4 million; and by 1911, had reached 45.3 million. At the same time, an increasing number of people lived in the towns. In 1801 22 per cent of the population was urban. In 1851 the proportion had reached 50 per cent and by 1901 it hit 77 per cent. Britain was not only the first *industrial* nation; it was also the first *urban* nation.

The cities of mid-Victorian Britain were therefore the product of an entirely new and explosive growth process. To take one example: the population of Liverpool grew from 82,000 in 1801 to 472,000 in 1861. It is not at all surprising, therefore, that living conditions in such cities were appalling, and could be catastrophic, as during the cholera outbreak of 1848, in which just over 13,000 Londoners died. Killer diseases could strike at both rich and poor – Prince Albert, Queen Victoria's husband, died of typhoid fever in 1861.

Victorian cities often contained fine new buildings, such as the great town halls constructed by the wealthy businessmen of Leeds and Huddersfield. But terrible problems existed in areas of cheap housing which had been hastily constructed to accommodate workers and migrants. In industrial towns it was common to construct long terraces of 'back-to-backs', with limited water supplies and primitive sewage disposal such as earth closets or cess-pits (holes in the ground into which sewage was poured). Such building might take place on cheap land which was poorly drained, or in smoky, heavily polluted areas around factories or near railway yards. The sheer numbers of people who crowded into these terraces simply added to the problems of dirt and disease, whilst poor building standards would add to the hazards. In other cities, such as London, the poorest housing might take the form of blocks of tenements surrounding a central courtyard, again with the most primitive sanitation. The middle classes, of course, avoided such areas and set up home in the expanding suburbs, for example Neasden and Dollis Hill on the edge of London, where they would lead 'respectable' domestic lives, often with the help of two or more servants.

Edwin Chadwick's *Report on the Sanitary Condition of the Labouring Population* in 1842 made it clear that conditions in the cities of Victorian Britain were a threat to life itself. He found that the average length of life of a labourer in the rural county of Rutland was 38 years (short enough by our standards) but that the average length of life of a labourer in Manchester was only 17 years! One has to be careful with such average figures, which can be misleading, but the situation was clear.

It is not difficult to explain why the levels of mortality were so high. Death was caused by disease, malnutrition, damp, cold, violence and lack of knowledge – to take an example, cholera spreads in sewage. Sewage escaped from cess-pits into the wells which were often the only source of drinking water. Such drains or sewers as existed often emptied into rivers such as the Thames, from which domestic water supplies were taken. The Thames was so polluted with sewage that during the 'Great Stink' of summer 1858, the House of Commons had to abandon its sitting!

However, by the middle of the nineteenth century, the process of improving the cities was already underway. In 1835 the Municipal Corporations Act gave 200 new and properly elected town councils the power to introduce improvements such as street lighting (using coal gas) and paving. Men such as Dr Southwood-Smith, Dr Kay Shuttleworth and Edwin Chadwick started to collect information about the plight of city-dwellers. In 1839 the Health of Towns Association was formed by Chadwick, Southwood-Smith, Disraeli and Shaftesbury. In 1846 the Bath- and Wash-houses Act permitted Councils to build bath-houses for the poor. The 1848 Public Health Act established the General Board of Health for London, and made it possible to set up similar boards in other cities. Then in 1854 Dr Snow plotted the cases of cholera on a map of London and showed that the victims were clustered around particular sources of water supply; he correctly concluded that cholera is transmitted through contaminated water. When in 1858 the stink of sewage in the Thames became so bad that Parliament had to be suspended, an Act was passed under which Joseph Bazalgette constructed two great sewerage systems for London, north and south of the river. In 1866 the Sanitary Act went further and required local authorities to ensure decent water supplies and sewage disposal.

Progress was piecemeal until the Conservative government of Benjamin Disraeli established the Local Government Board in 1871, to supervise the work of all local councils. Then in 1875 Disraeli passed the Public Health Act which brought together all the existing laws and required all cities to follow the example of Liverpool by appointing a Medical Officer of Health. At the same time, local councils were gaining powers to set building standards, and under the 1875 Artisans' Dwellings Act, councils could condemn buildings which were insanitary.

Consequently there were signs that conditions were getting better. The annual death rate in England and Wales fell after 1841, from about 23 per thousand to about 12 per thousand by the end of the century. Between 1873 and 1876 Birmingham was 'parked, paved, assized [law-courts introduced], marketed, gas-and-watered' under the leadership of its Mayor, Joseph Chamberlain, a member of the Liberal Party. There was still a huge amount to do, but the material benefits of being the Workshop of the World were starting to reach the people.

The Laying of the Water main in Tottenham Court Road, London (George Scharf). *Water contamination was the major cause of the spread of diseases such as cholera.*

VICTORIAN CITIES

Conditions in Victorian Cities

Manchester

The cottages are old, dirty, and of the smallest sort, the streets uneven, fallen into ruts, and in parts without drains or pavement; masses of refuse, offal, and sickening filth lie among standing pools in all directions; the atmosphere is poisoned with the effluvia [bad smells] from these, laden and darkened by the smoke of a dozen tall factory chimneys. A hoarde of ragged women and children swarm about here, as filthy as the swine that thrive upon the garbage heaps and in the puddles . . .

But what must one think when one hears that in each of these pens, containing at most two rooms, a garret, and perhaps a cellar, on the average twenty human beings live; that in the whole region, for each one hundred and twenty persons, one usually inaccessible privy is provided?

(Friedrich Engels *Conditions of the Working Class in England*, 1844)

Stockton

Shepherd's Buildings consist of two rows of houses with a street seven yards wide between them; each row consists of what are styled back and front houses – that is two houses placed back to back. There are no yards or out-conveniences; the privies are in the centre of each row, about a yard wide . . .

. . . each house consists of two rooms, viz., a house place and a sleeping-room above; each room is about three yards wide and four long . . . There are forty-four houses in the two rows, and twenty-two cellars, all of the same size. The cellars are let off as separate dwellings; these are dark, damp, and very low, not more than six feet between the ceiling and the floor.

The street between the two rows is seven yards wide, in the centre of which is the common gutter, or more properly sink, into which all sorts of refuse is thrown; it is a foot in depth. Thus there is always a quantity of putrefying matter [decaying rubbish] contaminating the air . . .

(Edwin Chadwick, *Sanitary Condition of the Labouring Population*, 1842)

Q

What do the scenes described by Engels and Chadwick both have in common?

CHECK YOUR UNDERSTANDING

Make a list of reasons why the living conditions of the urban poor were so bad.

Make another list of reasons why it was difficult to bring about improvements.

CAN YOU REMEMBER ?

Who was one of the most famous campaigners for improvements in living conditions?

What major Acts of Parliament started the process of improvement?

THINGS TO DO

1 Find out how a modern waterworks makes water fit for drinking.

2 Find out the causes of cholera and typhoid, and how they can be prevented.

3 Compare the problems of Victorian cities with the problems of cities in the developing world nowadays.

The Problem of Water Supply

A cartoon from *Punch* 1850

A DROP OF LONDON WATER.

Q

What did the cartoonist think was wrong with London's water? Was this cartoon drawn before or after the establishment of a proper scientific explanation of the causes of disease?

CONDITIONS IN THE FACTORIES

Working in a factory meant working continuously at the pace dictated by the machinery. It required starting work at a particular time of day and carrying on until the shift was finished. All of this was hard for the early generations of industrial workers, who had previously worked in agriculture or in their own homes. Consequently, discipline was harsh. Adult workers were fined heavily even for minor offences such as whistling or leaving a candle burning. Child workers, employed because they were cheap and because their parents needed the money, might be beaten with sticks or whips. Workplaces were dangerous: machinery was unguarded, ventilation and lighting were poor and the air was full of dust or fibres, giving rise to various industrial diseases.

Perhaps the worst aspect of working life in Britain during the early part of the nineteenth century, was the employment of children. For example, at the age of four, a child might be employed as a trapper, opening and shutting the traps or shutters which directed air through a coalmine. Orphans were sold as 'apprentices' to employers in the textile industry. Parents acted as labour sub-contractors, putting their own offspring to work in the mills. Perhaps most notorious of all, the rapidly multiplying chimneys of Victorian England were swept by climbing boys who were frequently crippled, killed or suffered from skin cancers caused by soot and dirt. However, it should be remembered that children had always been expected to work; the modern idea of childhood simply did not exist among the working classes.

Doing something to improve these conditions required action and agitation by reformers, men such as Michael Sadler, Richard Oastler and, most famous of all, Lord Shaftesbury. When he was a boy, Shaftesbury attended Harrow School and it is said that he witnessed the sorry spectacle of a pauper's funeral, whereupon he decided to devote his life to helping the poor and the abused. As Lord Ashley, he entered Parliament in 1826, and he succeeded to the title of Earl of Shaftesbury in 1851. He campaigned throughout his life for the relief of women and children who worked in mines and in factories. In particular he wanted to stop the use of climbing boys for sweeping chimneys. Even so, Shaftesbury was not sentimental, nor was he a socialist or a radical. As an Evangelical Christian he believed that the

working conditions in the mines and factories produced immoral and ignorant people, but as an aristocrat he believed that the working classes should still know their place in society. Shaftesbury died in 1885, the outstanding name in mid-nineteenth century reform.

To back up their campaigns, the reformers needed to make public the working conditions in the factories and mines. In 1831 Sadler was appointed chairman of a House of Commons committee to

investigate child labour. In 1832 he was able to shock MPs by revealing that children in Bradford were worked harder than slaves in the West Indies. Oastler referred to it as 'Yorkshire Slavery'. A Royal Commission was subsequently set up and its report was the basis of the 1833 Factory Act. Leadership of the movement for the protection of workers then shifted to Lord Ashley, and in 1842 the First Report of the Children's Employment Commissioners revealed to the public the terrible conditions in which women and children worked in the

coal mines. A second report by the Commission appeared in 1843, dealing with conditions in factories. The 1842 report resulted in the passing of the Coal Mines Act, and the 1843 Commission contributed to the passing of the 1844 Factory Act. The Commission continued to report on other trades and industries; for example, in 1863, it made public the way in which workers who made matches suffered from phosphorus poisoning, which ate away their jaws and nose cartilages. The Factory Acts Extension Act followed in 1864.

What protection did the growing number of laws give to working people? Early laws had set out to prevent the exploitation of orphans by mill owners (Health and Morals of Apprentices Act 1802) and to forbid the employment of children under nine in cotton mills, whilst restricting the hours of work of children between nine and sixteen to twelve hours per day (Factory Act 1819). However, it was the Factory Act of 1833 which (in addition to further reducing working hours for children in all factories) provided a way of enforcing the law. Government inspectors were appointed to ensure that the Act was carried out. Nevertheless the campaigners were not yet satisfied; their target was a ten-hour working day for all workers. The next step forward was the Coal Mines Act of 1842 which banned the employment underground of all women and girls, and of boys below the age of ten. Again, inspectors were appointed to ensure that the laws were observed.

As Britain was moving towards becoming the Workshop of the World, so the pace of reform quickened. The 1844 Factory Act established a 12-hour working day (nine on Saturdays) for women and young people under 18. Children under 13 could work a maximum of six-and-a-half hours in a day, leaving three hours for compulsory education. The Act also said that dangerous machinery had to be guarded. The Ten Hour Act of 1847 finally reduced the working hours of women and young people in textile mills to a maximum of ten hours a day. The ten-hour day for all workers in textile mills was achieved, more or less, in 1850.

Child factory labourers often worked for up to 18 hours a day, in atrocious conditions.

CONDITIONS IN THE FACTORIES

The Workshop of the World saw the conditions of its workers improving. However, working life was still hard and dangerous by modern standards. Unscrupulous employers would try to avoid the terms of the new laws, and even the employees themselves might want to work for longer hours than the law permitted. Fatal and crippling accidents were frequent, especially in heavy industry, and a cartoon in *Punch* at the time of the Great Exhibition reminded readers of the distressed condition of workers in 'sweated' trades such as clothing manufacture.

Working Conditions at Their Worst?

The following extract is taken from Oastler's letter on 'Yorkshire Slavery', written to the *Leeds Mercury* on 30 September 1830.

> **Thousands of little children, both male and female, but principally female from seven to fourteen years of age, are daily compelled to labour from six o'clock in the morning to seven in the evening, with only . . . thirty minutes allowed for eating and recreation. Poor infants, you are sacrificed at the shrine of avarice [extreme greed] . . . you are compelled to work as long as the necessity of your needy parents may require, or the cold blooded avarice of your worse than barbarian masters may demand . . . You are doomed to labour from morning to night for one who cares not how soon your weak and tender frames are stretched to breaking.**

Sum up Oastler's description of the condition of workers in the Yorkshire Worsted (woollen cloth) industry. Why do you think Oastler talked about 'Yorkshire *Slavery*' in his letter to the press?

THINGS TO DO

1 Find out more about the life and work of Lord Shaftesbury, and especially about 'climbing boys'.

2 Imagine you are a child working in the textile industry and write an account of your day.

3 Read the parts in *Oliver Twist* by Charles Dickens in which the orphan Oliver is to be apprenticed to various tradesmen, including a chimney sweep. Also look at *The Water Babies*, by Charles Kingsley.

CAN YOU REMEMBER ?

What hardships did climbing boys suffer?

What were the main acts which regulated the hours and conditions of factory workers?

A Factory Inspector Calls

Under which Act were the first Factory Inspectors appointed?
What do you think was their purpose?
Imagine the dialogue that might be going on between this Factory Inspector and these mill girls in Leeds.

The Worker is Not Yet Secure

Widespread unemployment was common during the American Civil War (1861–5) when there was a shortage of American raw cotton. The extract below is from the diary of John Ward, in the possession of the Historic Association of Lancashire and Cheshire.

> The mill I work in was stopped all last winter during which time I had three shillings per week allowed by the relief committee which barely kept me alive. When we started work again it was with Surat cotton, and a great number of weavers can only mind two looms. We can earn very little. I have not earned a shilling a day this last month and there are many like me . . . The principal reason why I did not write any notes this last two years is because I was sad and weary. One half the time I was out of work, the other I had to work as hard as ever I wrought [worked] in my life and can hardly keep myself living . . . I can't go much further with what I am at.

(quoted in John Addy, *The Textile Revolution*)

What difficulties has John Ward had to face and why?

Why should it be such a hardship for him to be out of work, and why does he then complain of being so busy?

What do you think Surat cotton is?

CHECK YOUR UNDERSTANDING

Why might newly-arrived workers in the first factories have found it difficult to come to terms with their work and environment?

Why were children employed in factories and mines?

Refer to the chapter on 'Self Help'. Would unskilled factory workers have been able to improve their conditions through Self Help, or would they need the assistance of laws made by Parliament? Discuss this with other members of your class.

The period 1873 to 1896 saw a decline in the prices that industry and agriculture could charge for their products and a reduction in the profits that could be made. In Parliament, serious worries were expressed that Britain was experiencing a 'Great Depression'. Competition, in particular from Germany and the United States, was hitting producers for the first time. Although most modern historians think that this was not really a depression – it was just that other countries were catching up – the self-confidence of the mid-Victorians was shaken and Britain's position as the Workshop of the World was coming to an end.

American output of steel rapidly caught up with British output during the 1870s and then overtook it in the early 1880s. By 1900 the United States produced about twice as much steel as Britain. German and British steel output rose at roughly the same rates until the mid-1890s, when German output overtook the British and continued to grow, whilst the British rate of growth flattened out. American coal production grew at a more rapid rate than that of Britain, and again overtook British output in the mid to late 1890s. German coal output did not exceed British output in the period we are considering, but the German rate of growth was higher and output was catching up because of more rapid mechanization. The productivity of German and American workers was also growing more

rapidly than that of the British, and the overall growth rate of manufacturers in Germany and the United States was faster than that of Britain, although Britain remained the most important producer of woollen and cotton textiles.

The reasons for Britain being 'overtaken' were complex. Germany and the United States had larger domestic populations to whom they could sell their goods. The United States in particular had greater natural resources. The Germans were better educated and more technologically aware. British management was slow to adopt new techniques and discoveries, whilst the Germans and Americans could benefit from the lessons of Britain's early experiences of industrialization.

There were clear signs of difficulties in agriculture as well. Poor harvests during the early 1870s had caused a rise in British grain prices just at the time when the new American railroads and transatlantic steam ships were starting to deliver vast amounts of cheap grain from the recently settled prairies. British grain farmers were dramatically undercut; American grain arriving on the dockside in Liverpool was cheaper than British grain, and prices fell from an average of £2.37 per quarter between 1875–9 to £1.35 between 1900–4.

British meat and wool producers experienced similar competition. In the United States, the invention of barbed wire and the resumption of westward movement after the Civil War resulted in the fencing of huge areas of grassland for the grazing of beef cattle, and the development of refrigerator ships made it possible to transport meat overseas. Clipper ships could carry wool from Australia. The world market in agricultural goods was changing rapidly, and Britain had abandoned protection against foreign farmers in 1846 (see page 8). Wheat producers were especially hard hit, and the numbers employed in agriculture fell from 1.6 million in 1871 to 1.3 million in 1901.

One of the most obvious signs of Britain's changing position in world trade was the presence of foreign-made articles in the shops. In particular, German toys and metal goods attracted almost hysterical criticism. But it would be incorrect to imagine that everything was now going wrong for the Workshop of the World. Britain's economy *was* still growing – more goods, more coal, and more iron were being produced. British merchant ships still dominated the trade routes of the world. It was just that other countries were now starting to produce more, or perhaps were producing more efficiently in newer factories. At the same time, those British people who were in work could buy more because of cheaper prices; consequently the 1880s and 1890s were a period of rapid urban growth and expansion in the retail trade, when companies such as W.H. Smiths and Boots grew to national importance.

The speed at which the output of German steel factories like this grew in the 1890s was one of the causes of the 'depression' of British trade.

Agricultural Depression

Whatever differences of opinion may exist as to the causes of agricultural depression or as to remedies which may be suggested for it . . . there prevails complete uniformity of conviction as to the great extent and intensity of the distress which has fallen on the agricultural community. The two most prominent causes for that distress are bad seasons and foreign competition, aggravated by the increased cost of production and the heavy losses of livestock. Whereas formerly the farmer was to some extent compensated by a higher price for a smaller yield, he has had in recent years to compete with an unusually large supply at greatly reduced prices.

(From a report by Her Majesty's Commission on Agriculture, 1882, quoted in P.J. Larkin, *English Economic and Social History*)

What does this report identify as the reasons for the depression in agriculture?

Why were farmers in other parts of the world now able to compete so fiercely with British farmers?

Were British farmers sensible to have concentrated so much on growing wheat since 1846?

German Competition

The toys, and the dolls, and the fairy books which your children maltreat in the nursery are made in Germany; nay, the material of your favourite (patriotic) newspaper had the same birthplace as like as not. Roam the house over, and the fatal mark will greet you at every turn, from the piano in your drawing room to the mug on your kitchen dresser . . . Descend to your domestic depths, and you shall find your very drain-pipes German-made.

(From E.E. Williams' pamphlet 'Made in Germany', 1896, quoted in R.B. Jones *Economic and Social History of England 1770–1977*.)

What is E.E. Williams' attitude towards German goods?

What measures might he have suggested to combat German competition?

THINGS TO DO

1 Look back at the chapters on iron and steel and on machine tools and engineering. Suggest reasons why the United States and Germany pulled ahead in steel production.

2 Name an industry in which Britain still dominated the world.

3 Find a book in your library which tells the story of the settlement and economic growth of the United States from the end of the American Civil War (1865).

CAN YOU REMEMBER ?

What are tariffs *and* protectionism*? Look at page 8 if you are not sure.*

What are the approximate dates of the 'Great Depression'?

CHECK YOUR UNDERSTANDING

Explain *real wages*. What might cause real wages to fall?

Why are statistics for steel and coal production helpful in understanding what was happening to the British economy?

Caught Napping

CAUGHT NAPPING !

Can you explain the meaning of this cartoon?

What do you think the cartoonist's attitude was to both Britain and Germany?

The following rhyme was printed beneath this cartoon when it was published:

There was an old lady as I've heard tell,
She went to market her goods to sell,
She went to market on a market day
And she fell asleep on the world's highway.
By came a pedlar – German – and stout,
And he cut her petticoats all round about!

What can you remember?

Do you know?

Why Britain was called the Workshop of the World?

Why the Great Exhibition was important?

What problems the inhabitants of industrial towns faced in Victorian Britain?

How did the railways affect technology, and what were the other effects of the railway revolution?

What were the advantages of steel?

Who published a book on Self Help, and what did it mean?

What improvements were made in the lives of ordinary people?

What was Lord Shaftesbury famous for?

In what ways Britain was no longer the Workshop of the World by the end of the nineteenth century?

TIME CHART

1830	Opening of the Liverpool and Manchester Railway.
1837	Queen Victoria comes to the throne.
1838	London and Birmingham Railway opened. First section of the Great Western Railway opened. *Sirius* and *Great Western* cross the Atlantic under steam power.
c1840–1875	The Golden Age of British Agriculture.
1839	James Nasmyth's steam hammer invented.
1843	Introduction of Joseph Whitworth's standardized screw threads.
1844	The Rochdale Pioneers.
1846	Repeal of the Corn Laws.
1851	The Great Exhibition. Census reveals that the UK is the first 'urban' nation, with half the population living in towns and cities.
1852–5 & 1859–66	W.E. Gladstone as Chancellor of the Exchequer completes the work of establishing Free Trade.
1856	Henry Bessemer's Converter.
1867	Second Parliamentary Reform Act.
1871	Gladstone's Trade Union Act. Whilst recognizing Trade Unions, the subsequent Criminal Law Amendment Act made it difficult for them to engage in organized action during a trade dispute.
1872	Introduction of the Secret Ballot.
1875	Disraeli's Conspiracy and Protection of Property Act makes it lawful for Trade Unions to take peaceful organized action in a trade dispute. Disraeli's Public Health Act. Disraeli's Artisans' Dwellings Act.
1876	Approximate onset of the Agricultural Depression and the 'Great Depression' in trade and industry.

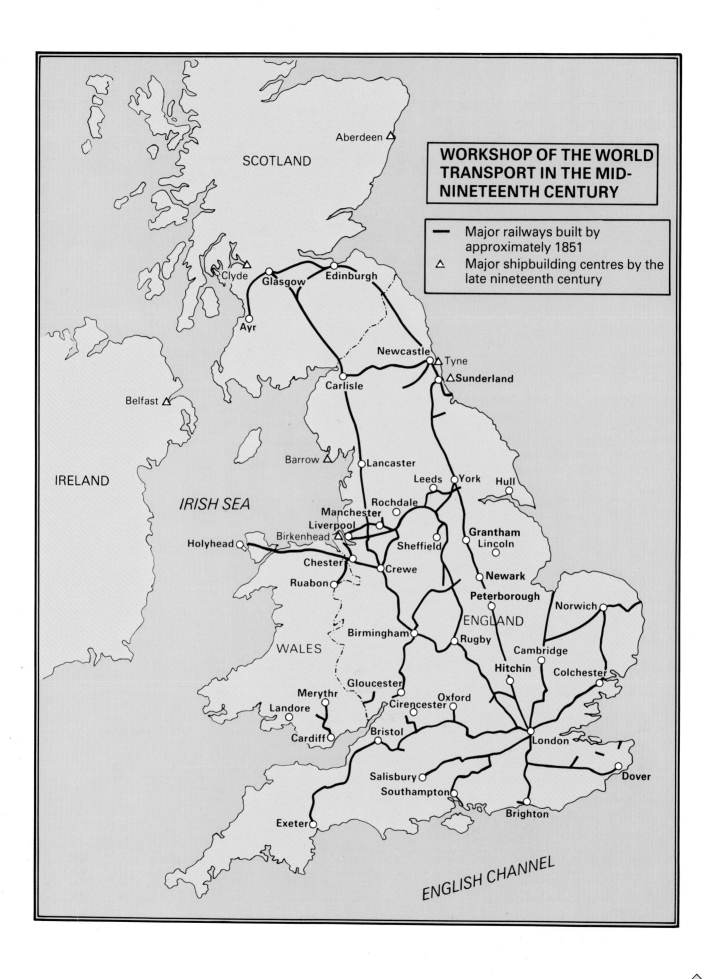

WORKSHOP OF THE WORLD
TRANSPORT IN THE MID-
NINETEENTH CENTURY

—— Major railways built by
approximately 1851

△ Major shipbuilding centres by the
late nineteenth century

SCOTLAND

Aberdeen △

Clyde △
Glasgow
Edinburgh

Ayr

Newcastle △ Tyne
△ Sunderland

Carlisle

Belfast △

IRELAND

Barrow △
Lancaster

IRISH SEA

Leeds York
Hull

Rochdale
Manchester
Liverpool
Birkenhead △

Sheffield

Grantham
Lincoln

Holyhead

Chester
Ruabon
Crewe

Newark

Peterborough

Norwich

ENGLAND

Birmingham
Rugby

Cambridge

WALES

Hitchin

Colchester

Merythr
Landore

Gloucester
Cirencester
Oxford

Cardiff

Bristol

London

Dover

Salisbury
Southampton

Brighton

Exeter

ENGLISH CHANNEL

45

GLOSSARY

back-to-backs   long terraces of houses, where the buildings back on to each other

birth-rate   a measure of the number of children being born over a given period, usually expressed as the number of births per thousand of the population per year

Board of Trade   the government department that looks after trade and manufacturing

cast iron, casting   is the process of making shaped objects by pouring liquid metal into a mould made of damp sand, and then allowing the metal to solidify, taking on the shape of the mould

clipper ships   very fast and elegant sailing ships, which carried the most precious and important cargoes from around the world to Britain until late in the nineteenth century; they were faster than many steam ships, did not have to stop for coal, and did not have to waste cargo space by carrying fuel

compound steam engine   a type of steam engine in which the steam is re-used, thereby saving fuel

Co-op, Co-operative Society   a shop or organization for manufacturing or selling goods, to which the customers can belong, the profits being either shared among the customers or invested in the society

Corn Law   a law made in 1815 which placed an import duty on foreign wheat or other grains entering the country

death-rate   a measure of the number of people dying over a given period, usually expressed as the number of dead per thousand of the population per year

democracy   a form of government in which all the people take part in choosing the government

engineering
mechanical: the making of machines
civil: the construction of roads, bridges etc.
electrical: the construction of electrical machines and electrical systems

exports   goods and articles sold to other countries

fertilizer   a substance added to the soil to make crops grow faster or larger

franchise   the right to vote in elections

Free Trade   a policy of allowing goods into and out of the country without paying any customs duties

imports   goods and articles brought into the country from abroad

lathe   a machine tool for shaping metal or wood by turning it and bringing a cutting edge to bear against it

malleable   capable of being bent and shaped

mass-production   production of large numbers of items which are all made to exactly the same dimensions and specifications

milling machine   a machine tool for cutting grooves or machining flat surfaces on metal

Parliament   a body of elected representatives of the people who make the laws of the land and from which the government is chosen

protection, protectionism   the policy of protecting factory owners or farmers from foreign competition and imports, by means of imposing tariffs or import duties

puddling   a process for making a malleable form of iron, called wrought iron, by re-heating it and stirring it in a furnace

Punch   a humorous magazine, well-known for its cartoons on the politics and issues of the day

reaper   machine for cutting cereal crops such as wheat

reform   process of changing things for the better

secret ballot   voting in secret, so that nobody can tell which way any individual person voted

seed drill   machine for sowing seeds

sub-contracting   a process in which an employer breaks a job down into separate parts, and then pays other employers or companies to undertake those separate parts of the work

tariffs   taxes or customs duties levied on goods entering or leaving the country

tenements   buildings subdivided into many different dwellings and containing large numbers of people

threshing   the process of removing grain such as wheat or barley from the stems on which it has grown, by beating by hand or machine

Trade Union   an organization or association of workers from a particular trade or industry, who join together to bargain with their employers over wages or conditions of work

For younger readers

R.J. Cootes, *Britain since 1700*, Longman, 1982

J. Chisholm, *The Nineteenth Century*, Usborne, 1992

John Ray and James Hagerty, *The Course of British History 3*, Hutchinson, 1987

Longman's *Then and There* series: *London Life and the Great Exhibition, Edwin Chadwick, Poor Law and Public Health, The Railway Revolution*

For older readers

J.D. Chambers, *The Workshop of the World*, O.U.P. 1961

C.P. Hill, *British Economic and Social History*, Edward Arnold 1977

G. Martin Guest, *A Brief History of Engineering*, Harrap 1974

R.B. Jones, *Economic and Social History of England, 1770–1977*, Longman 1977

Denis Richards and J.W. Hunt, *An Illustrated History of Modern Britain, 1783–1980*, Longman, fifth impression 1991

Philip Sauvain, *British Economic and Social History (Book One: 1700–1870; Book Two: 1850 to the Present Day)*, Stanley Thornes, 1987

Acknowledgements

The Author and Publishers would like to thank the following for their kind permission to reproduce illustrations: The Mary Evans Picture Library for pages 1, 4, 5, 6, 9, 10, 15, 18, 19, 21, 22, 23, 24, 25, 26, 30, 31, 36, 37, 38 and 39; The Bridgeman Art Library for pages 12, 13, 16, 33, 40 and 41; e.t. archive for pages 28 and 29; and K.S. Smith (illustrator) for the map on page 45.

The cover illustration shows *Iron and Coal* by William Bell Scott, and is reproduced by kind permission of the National Trust Photographic Library.

Thanks go to the *How It Was* series editors for advice and editorial input: Madeline Jones, Jessica Saraga and Michael Rawcliffe.

INDEX

Page numbers in **bold type** refer to illustrations.